I0494652

Yùgen

Copyright © 2016

By: Jamilah Tahirah Abdullah

Illustrated By: Jamilah Tahirah Abdullah

&

Latifa Abdul-Haqq

All rights are reserved. No part of this book may be reproduced in any form, except for the inclusion of brief quotations in review with citations, without permission in writing from the author and publisher.

ISBN #: 978-1537243405

Table of Contents

Dedicated to our loving mother,

Rashida.

Yùgen

Yùgen is transcendent beauty. Only the individual can experience Yùgen. A person can transcend into a spiritual realm.

Yùgen allows the doors of imagination to open. Yùgen is often described as mystery and depth.

Yùgen is a beauty behind the surface that exists on another plane of reality. A master work of art can take an individual there.

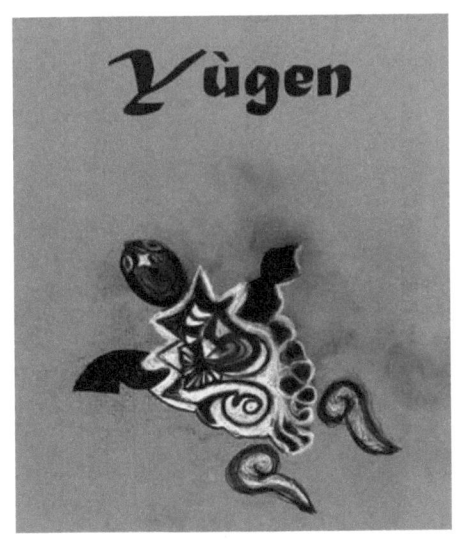

"Coming out of your shell"

Polynesian Turtle

By Jamilah Abdullah

Examples of Yùgen in Nature

The turtle is a good representation of Yùgen. The turtle, within her shell, knows herself deeply: what makes her blood pulse and when she is ready she comes out of her shell.

She explores the world around her, soaks up the sun and shares her being. Since the turtle carries her home with her, she is ready to go where life takes her. Life may be a mystery, but just like sea turtles find their way to the ocean, we have a hidden compass that will guide us to our ocean of life.

I find Yùgen in my life by first seeing the world as immensely beautiful. Nature is one of my greatest inspirations. Nature and animals bring a sense of peace and healing that I aim to translate through my art.

Examples of Yùgen in Nature (continued)

To face obstacles, such as negative voices or energy, I morph them into writing and art. (For example, *Skull Mist* shows the darkness swishing away with a new dawn.)

To find Yùgen in your own life, first find out what makes you feel truly alive and pursue that. Once you live your passion, you in turn experience and demonstrate the essence of your life. Your demonstration, in turn, is shared with everyone you encounter, thus spreading beauty throughout the world.

You may have to try different things before you find your passion, but that is part of the unfolding journey. You may choose to tell your story through dance, singing, painting or simply . . . being. The fruit produced is the essence of Yùgen.

Lucy The Elephant
By: Jamilah Abdullah

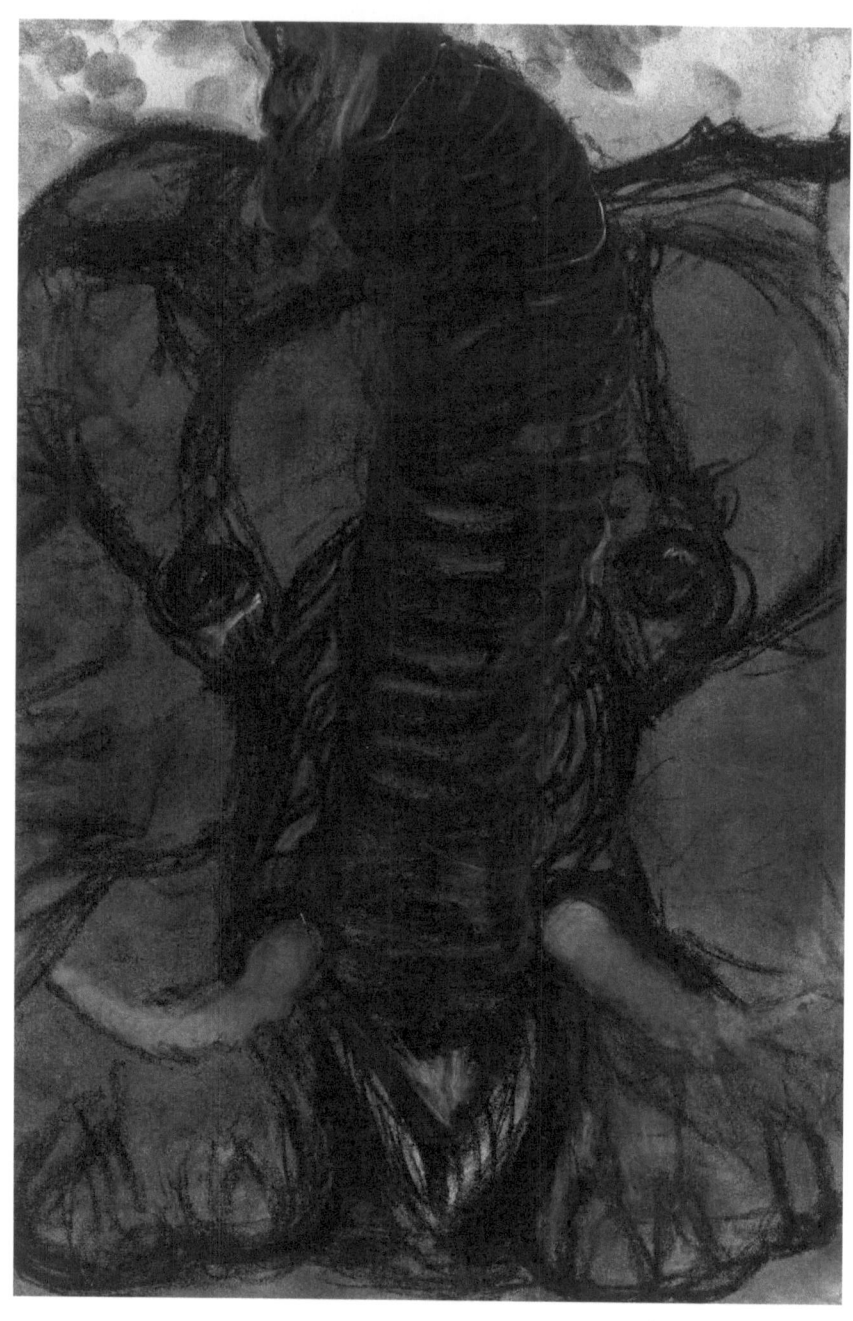

Visual Art

The healing nature of art is that

it evokes feelings and

allows us to feel the spectrum of

emotions in a safe environment.

As an artist,

my sister Latifa is

inspired by texture.

She likes the heightened sense of

feeling the world around us.

She loves to create layers in her art,

which reflect the layers

in our own characters.

As for my life

as an illustrator,

I am profoundly inspired by

nature and the sense of adventure it sparks.

Visual Art (continued)

Art can take you anywhere,

and that freedom is the true

beauty of imagination.

For both my sister and I,

we want people to get

the message they need to see

from the art pieces we

create.

Create Your Own Canvas
Reflective Pause:

Kneeling Woman
By: Latifa Abdul-Haqq

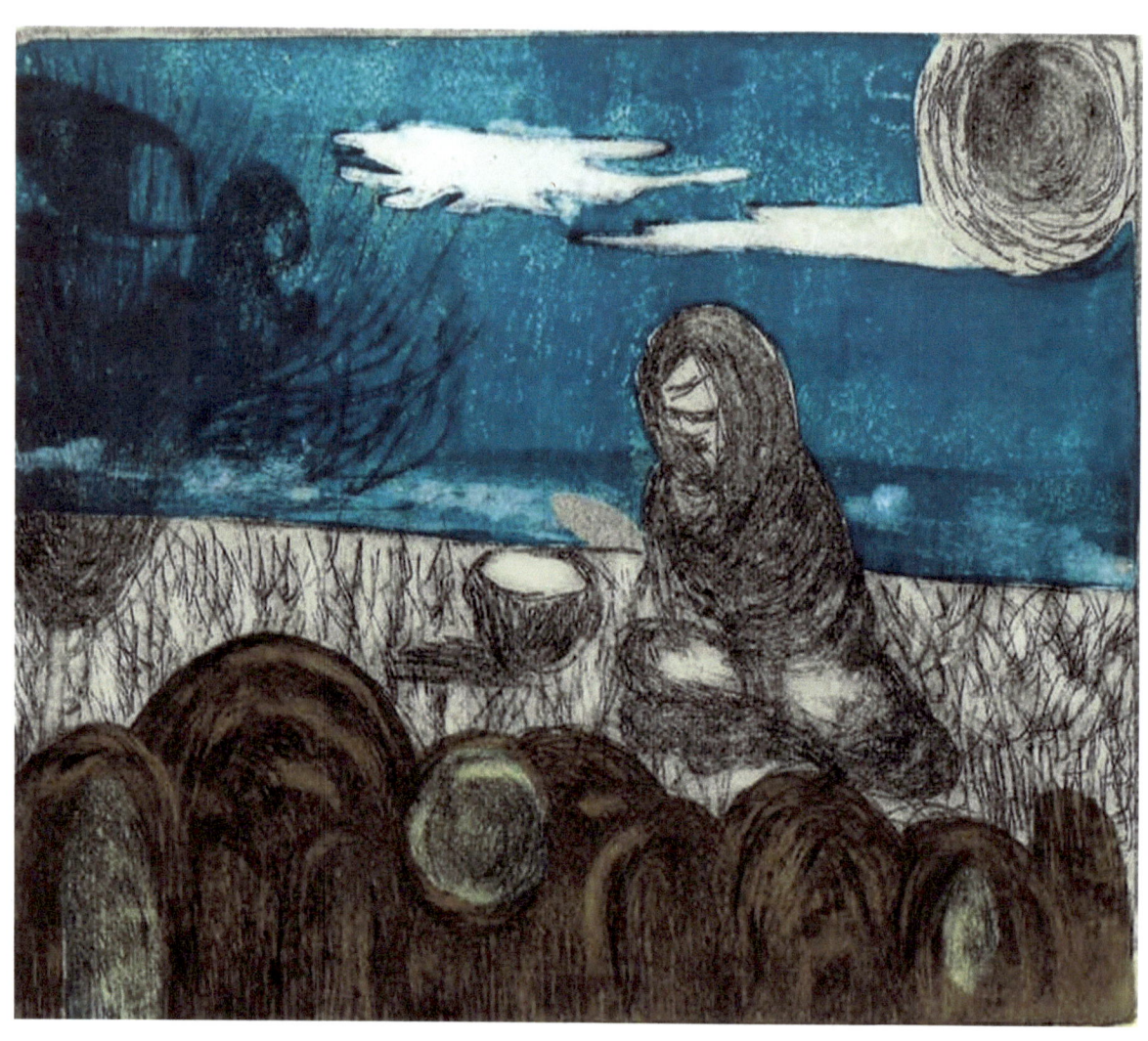

The Day That Gave

A subconscious memory lingers
This is a memory not settled upon imagery.
Memory is a knowledge that runs through my veins.

The water broke with the break of this day.
One spirit gave way to a life.
A subconscious memory lingers.

The numbers turned out to be 2/12/91
The name became Beautiful Pure Servant of God.
Memory is a knowledge that runs through my veins.

An identity came about.
This is the start.
A subconscious memory lingers.

Gaze upon gaze
Give upon take
Memory is a knowledge that runs through my veins.

She sees before her what she has nurtured.
She is now called a mother.
A subconscious memory lingers.
Memory is a knowledge that runs through my veins.

Explanation:

The break of a new day reflects my mother's water breaking and my life coming into play. This day was specially chosen for me to begin sowing the seeds to beautify the earth.

Each and every person has an identity as unique as their fingerprint and each person's destiny is a mystery. Through belief in a guiding force and in ourselves, we find clues that unlock that mystery.

What is YOUR *Day that Gave*?

What will you do with its significance?

_____

_____

_____

_____

_____

_____

_____

_____

Chained Heart

By: Latifa Abdul Haqq

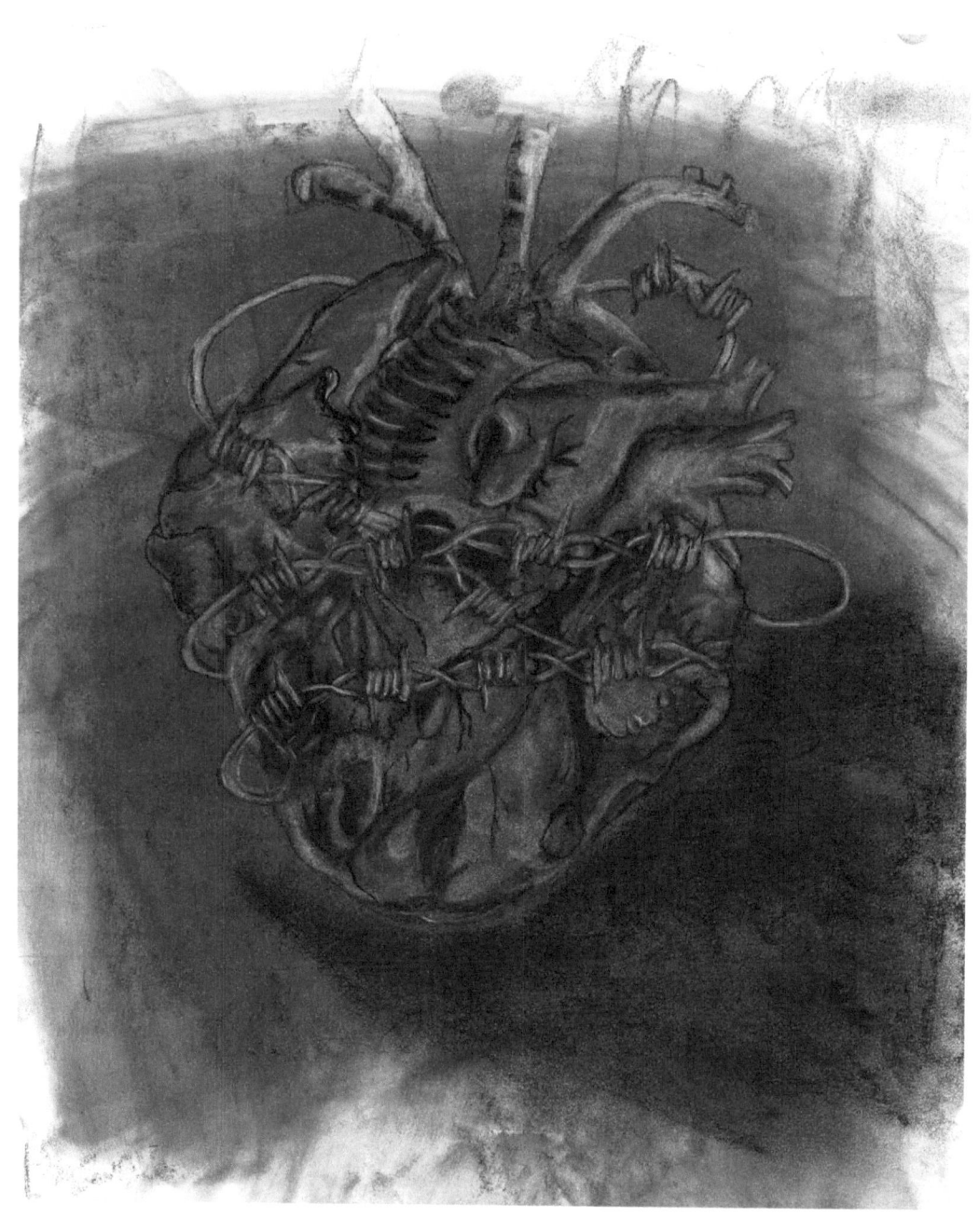

Canopy

Life is as the rolling of dice.
The heart needs to be guarded against
darkness ready to pounce.

Sometimes the chain around our heart
is so tight, we hurt ourselves.
Behind it all is a softness.

There shall be no mask of a clown
upon the face.
There will dwell freedom upon the wings
of a bird.

The skies clear up,
and so will the mind.
The rain of God's mercy prevails.

The needle no longer pokes through the thumbs
but sews robes of glory.

This poem was written and given to a jail inmate, as a source of hope and to help him avoid falling into despair. Hope is how we unchain our hearts; friendship is how we heal those wounds caused by the chains.

Water & Heaven

By: Latifa Abdul-Haqq

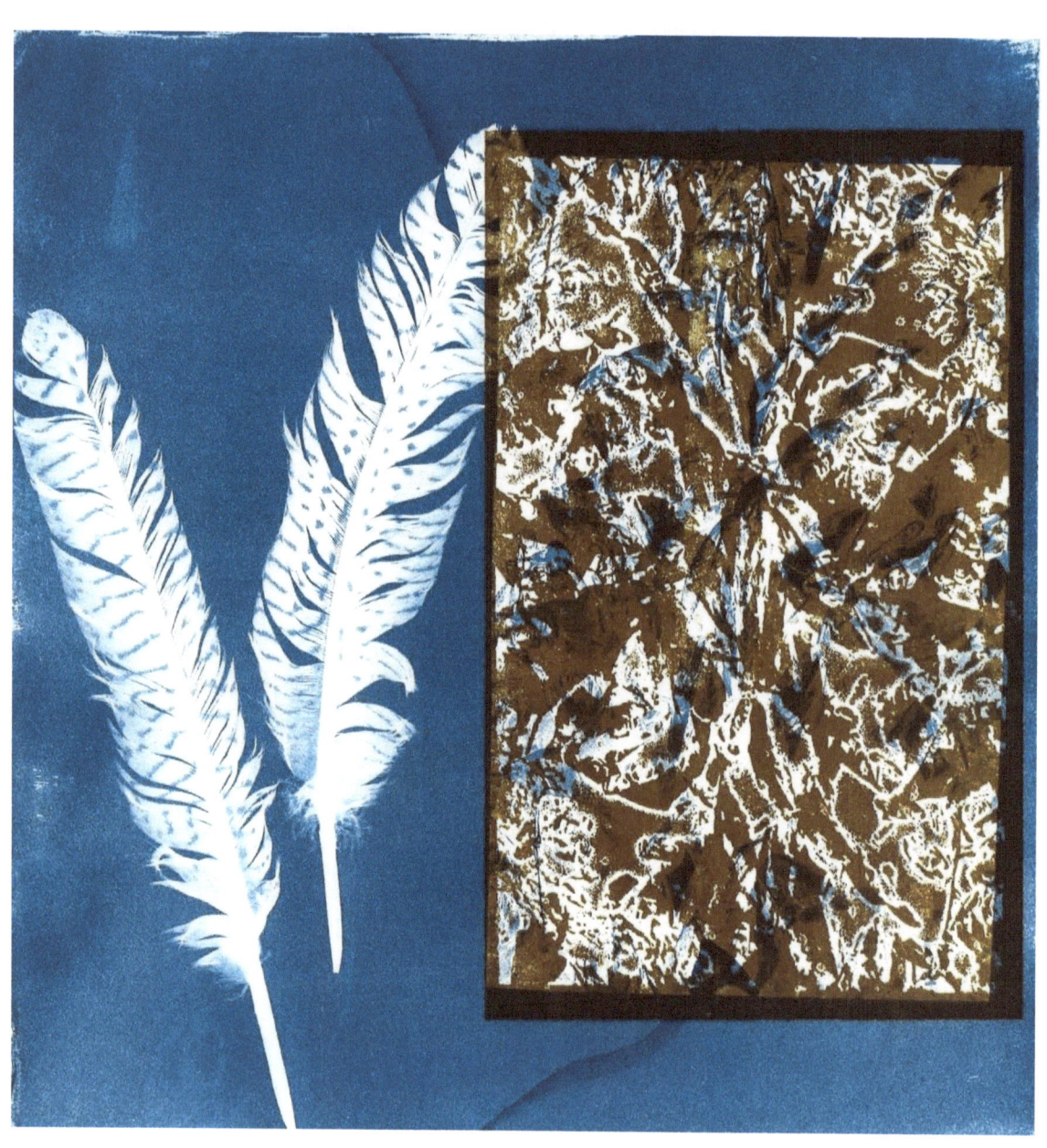

Orbit

There once lived a man and a woman who dwelled amongst the sky. They lived a life with no complications and they lived this way for a long time. The woman had an idea. She told the man that she would like to have something else in her life – a change.

The man grew hot with rage. He yelled at the woman, "Your life is so easy and you want more?" The man's body was shaking. Then, in an instant, he became a ball of fire.

The sky clouded up and the woman curled up into a ball. The woman wept and wept.

She stayed curled up in a ball so long that she could no longer stand up. Plant life began to sprout on her back. Humans and animals burst from her womb. She is called Mother Earth. The sun still rages, but it is calmer, some days more than others.

The other planets are aunts and uncles. The stars are cousins. The stars sometime come down to visit Mother Earth. Mother Earth's children sometimes visit their aunts and uncles. Diversity keeps Mother Earth spinning around the sun in her idea that came alive.

Explanation:

Nature sets an example of harmony.

Nature shows us how to function through an ecosystem. Individuals certainly should strive to improve their own life, but they need to keep a unified goal in mind as they work in societies and establish international relations.

The goal can start with a love for Mother Earth and out of love comes nurturing. Nature highlights that we each have something to contribute and need to work with one another. If we do not work together, then there is destruction and chaos.

What areas are out of balance in your life? What examples in nature would you rather have your life resemble?

_____

_____

_____

_____

_____

_____

_____

_____

Ancient Hand

By: Jamilah Abdullah

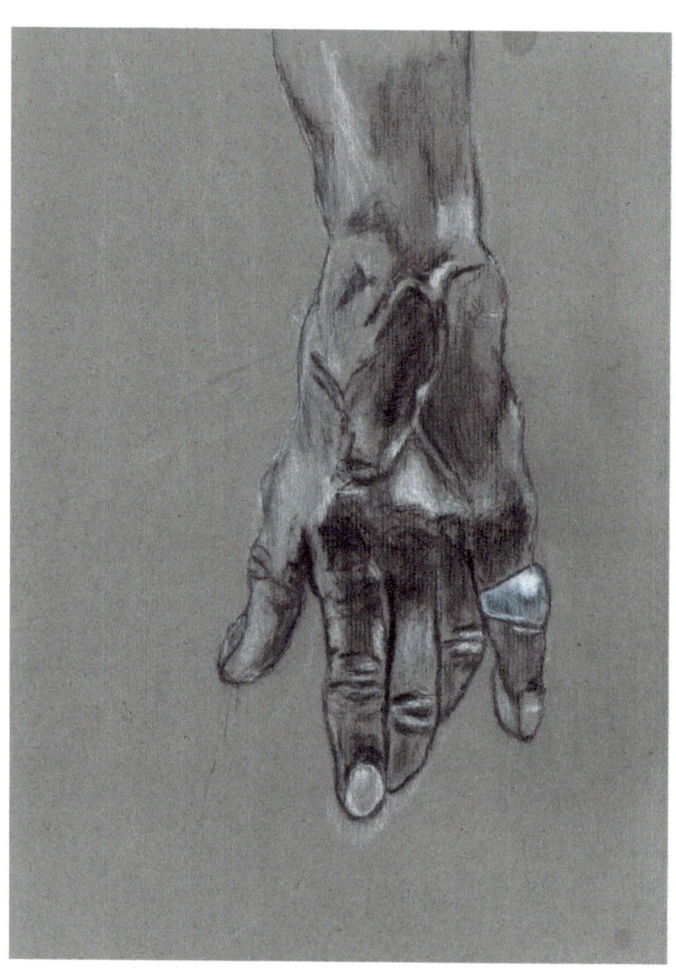

Ancestors

In the end, we are on our own journeys; we just meet each other
in passing.
The nature of Change is hard to grasp,
But
As we go
We leave a trail of footsteps as a guide
For those
We leave in the dust.

As the soul's energy disperses, material matter ceases to exist.
Some will be remembered through pages in a history book,
Or kept
Cherished in a locket of a descendant.
Now and then
Whispers of the wind will play nostalgic melodies on our
heartstrings,
And we shall honor
Those who marched to the sound of their own voices.

In loving memory of
Kathryn Israel
July 18, 2015

In the loving memory of Kathryn Israel
7/18/2015

The first time I saw the lady in a long red coat on the curb, I said to myself, "I would like to get to know her".

Kathryn Israel and I became instant friends. Actually, she became the grandma that I never got the chance to meet.

She shared stories, healing remedies and recipes with me. She lived with an all-white cat that was as fierce as her. She was witty and sharp.

Kathryn's life was an adventure like that of a true gypsy; she made up her own rules as she went. She had traveled all around the U.S. and never claimed to own a piece of the land. She belonged to the Apache tribe.

Her nickname for me was Luju, which means *wild dove*. We were two birds navigating through the stars.

Create Your Own Canvas
Reflective Pause:

Mayan Butterfly
By: Latifa Abdul-Haqq

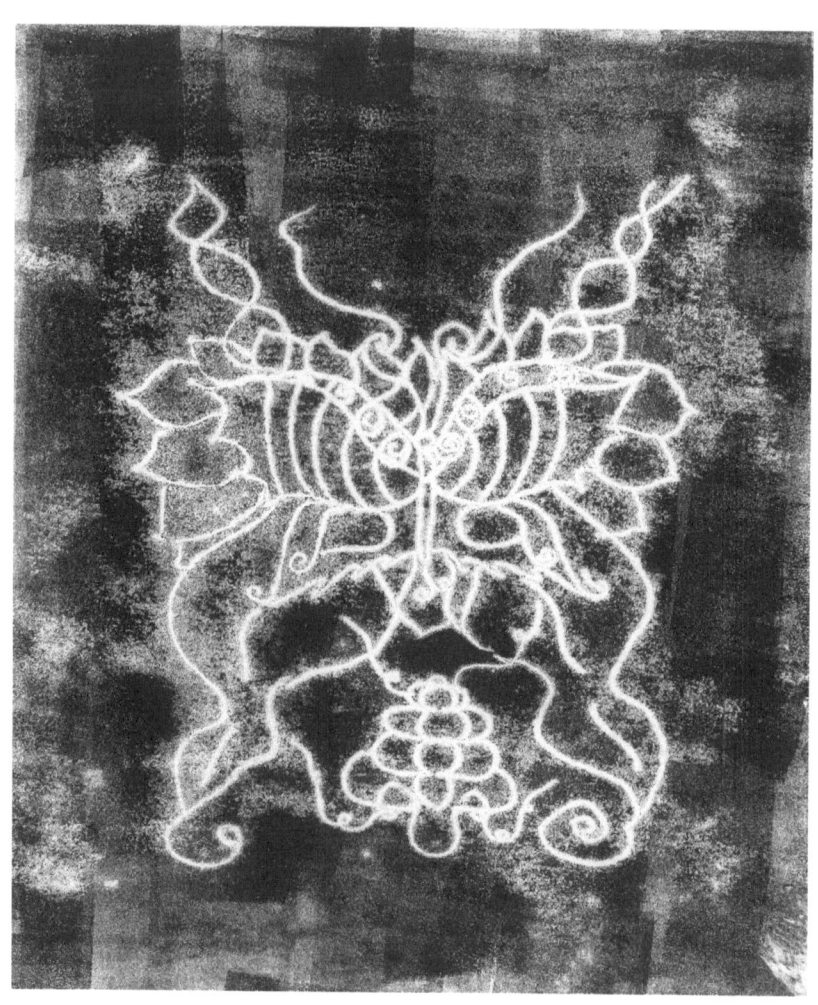

Stretching the Canvas

The dominating, light-skinned ones
captured the sweat
from the brown soil-like people of Mexico.

They used the sweat to grow
Their own worldly possessions
Under the word of religion.

Their arrogance crushed massive souls.
They made people feel as if
they were nothing more than dirt.

Whereas they had the right to troupe over others
The strong ones held onto their so-called
mud-stained hands
And made adobe with them
To knock out the clock of arrogance.

The rebels were pushed further down
into the ground.
There they sprouted
into millions of calla lilies.

Stretching the Canvas (continued)

They showed that Mexico's beauty will prevail
No matter how hard people try to destroy it
with their toxic harsh rule
of the cleaning out variety.

The canvas will be stretched
and the mind needs to be stretched.

The clay will be softened
to make a pot
that holds an understanding of variety in the world.

The fabulous Mexican Muralist Diego River inspired me to write this poem. His life size murals take me on a walk through the streets of Mexico. For me, growing up in New Mexico made me feel a part of Mexico's rich history.

Looking at many of today's troubling events, what groups of people do we need to reflect on to understand our current state?

_____

_____

_____

_____

_____

_____

_____

Lemon Landscape

By: Latifa Abdul-Haqq

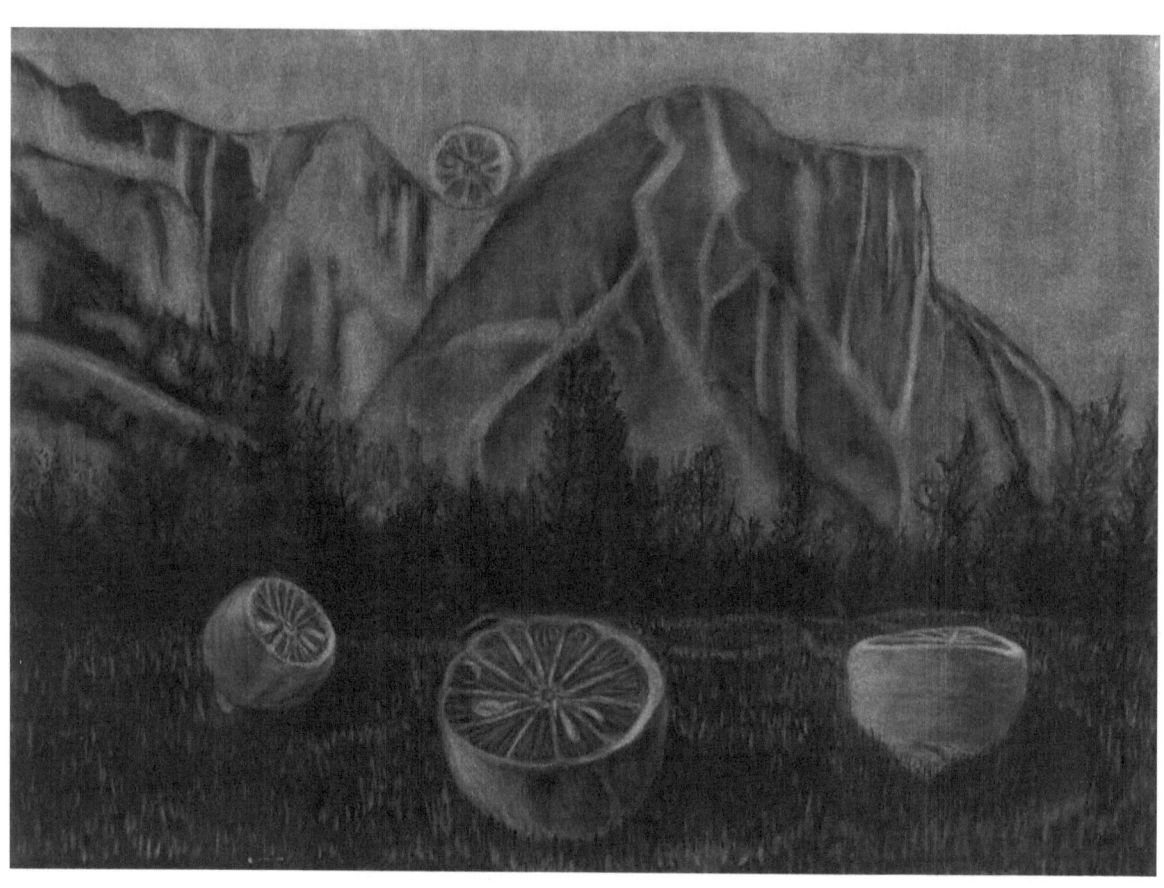

Pink The Sun

Umi always made the sun
pull the tea from the bags.
I ran circles around that jar,
as I watered the pink primroses.

Cooing called me to a pigeon egg hunt,
in between playing hide-and-seek
around the silver Mercury.

My mother yelled from the kitchen window,
telling me to button my tan jacket
with the buttons that said "Roxy".

As I swayed on the tire swing
watching my pink rubber sandals
shimmer as my feet went into sunlight
back into the shade of the cottonwood.

Branch by branch
Tree racing
As I reached the top
sunset spread
overlooking the train tracks.

Pink The Sun (continued)

Going to the neighbor's
to have the first taste
of bitter coffee.

Walking on the sidewalk
getting a drift of beans in the crockpot
and sopaipillas in the frying pan
calling me to the orange wool rug.

Create Your Own Canvas
Reflective Pause:

Young Lady

By: Jamilah Abdullah

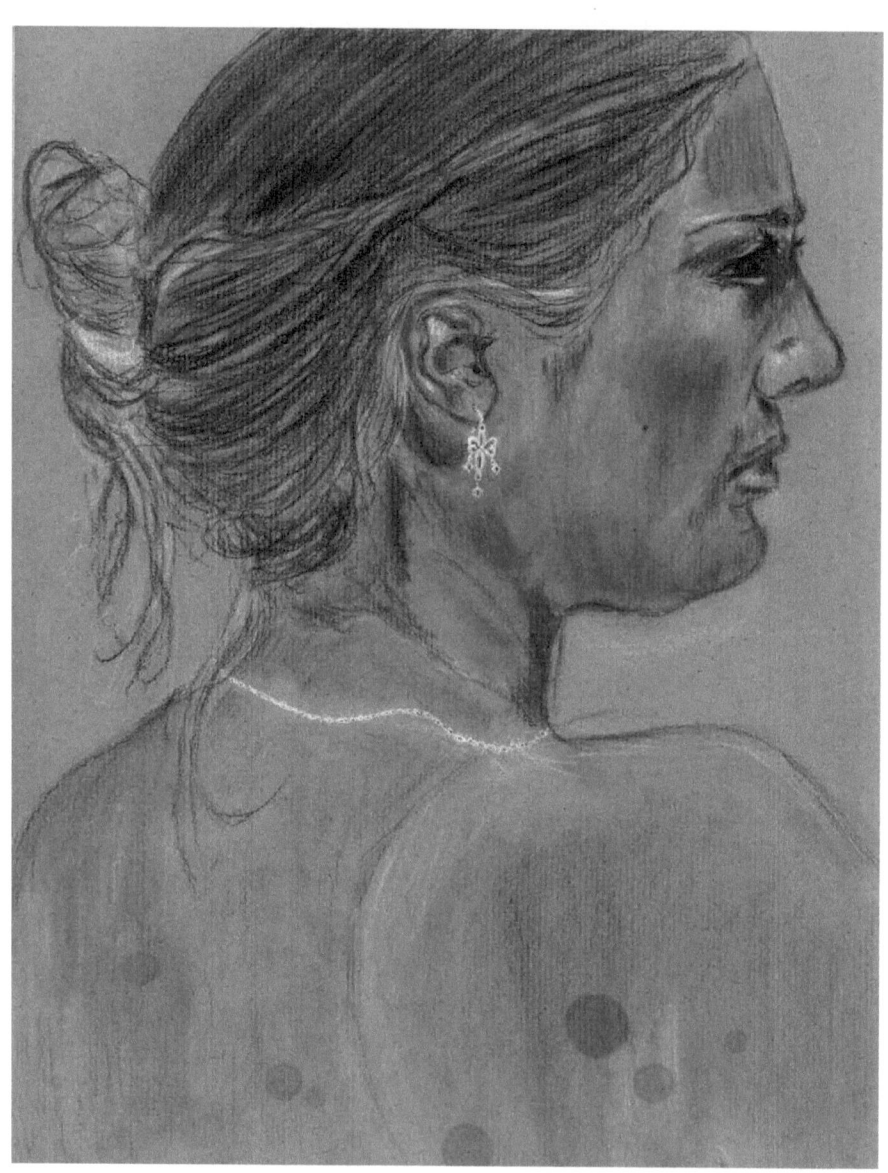

Little Sister

Holes will come along the path of good health.

Keep your eyes searching around the world.

Seal your shirt tight and protect your health.

Hold on with both hands, embracing high faith.

There will be many obstacles to unfold.

Holes will come along the path of good health.

Set out as wings of a moving moth.

Prance along the hills before your bones grow old.

Seal your shirt tight and protect your health.

Keep smiling, but realize what lies beneath.

Don't let your soul be sold for gold.

Holes will come along the path of good health.

Heed to the words that form from mother's mouth.

Be the sun in the middle of June – bold.

Seal your shirt tight and protect your health.

Little Sister (continued)

Be as pure as the egg white cloth.

Be cleanly – don't allow the form of mold.

Holes will come along the path of good health.

Seal your shirt tight and protect your health.

This poem reflects my older sister, Latifa, giving me advice about life. She is telling me to take care of myself, to stay healthy. She is telling me to be aware of my surroundings and the company I keep.

She is encouraging me to fly. She is also telling me to have fun while I am young. She is wishing me happiness and not to be bought by greed and materialism. She is telling me to listen to our mother's wise words. She is telling me to be sweet, yet strong. Lastly, she is telling me to be clean, which refers to remaining virtuous.

What is the best advice you've been given and by whom? How does it apply to your life today?

_____

_____

_____

_____

_____

_____

_____

_____

Illusion

By: Jamilah Abdullah

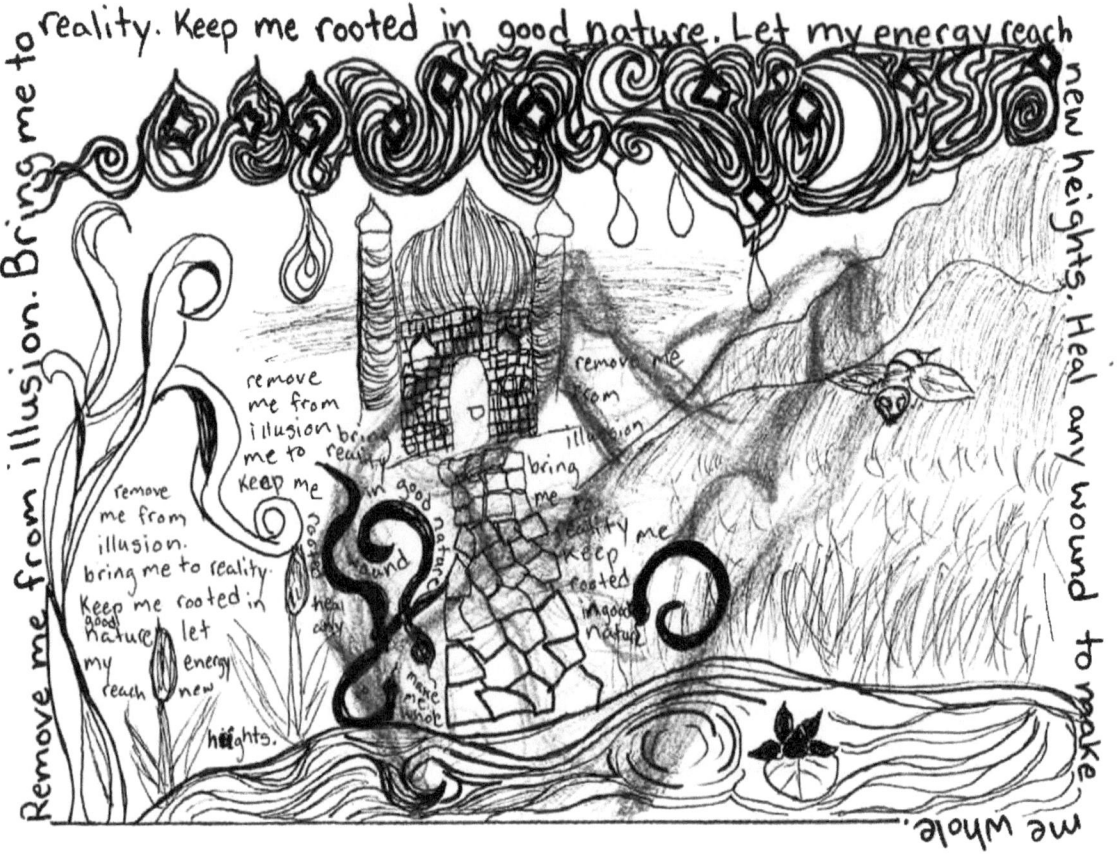

Artificial or Natural

What is real and what is fake? What is the difference between fake and real?

Fake is the external expression of an emotion without the inner meaning.

Fake is a mask that covers the face of what the person is feeling.

Fake is deception.

Faking everything is disconnection with the soul.

In order to make something real, the mind, body and soul all have to be engaged – all three affect one another.

When one element goes against another there is an imbalance. The spiritual heart is the soul. The heart is what pumps energy through the rest of the human structure.

The mind can be confused. The body can be sick. The soul can be broken. The soul is essential, for the soul is what holds sincerity.

When the soul breaks into a million glass pieces, then those pieces can rip up the mind and body. Real is beyond the body and beyond the material world.

Eating something toxic can also disturb the body. The poor actions of people may get them into bad situations but, their overall outlook, vibe or aura makes you feel good when you're around them.

Artificial or Natural (continued)

Things that spark the soul and inspire emotions cause the strongest reactions within the human being. Spirituality speaks to the soul. Being at prayer is the ultimate feeling of peace.

There is an art of controlling one's emotions. While striving to be a better person and to find wisdom, one is on the path of clearing the inner being. This process allows one's mind to become clear and his or her body to heal.

The mind is for soaking up knowledge and then sending that knowledge to the heart; only then can that knowledge be fashioned into wisdom.

The body is for the physical capacity and is the outer nervous system. The five senses engage in the world. The body is the letter that can send signals to us that tell us about the internal being.

The body is the transition from our own being in the world around us.

All people are born pure and good. After birth, a defect may happen to one's mind that results in mental health issues. The default could be doubt, which is caused by a weak connection between the heart, where the soul lives and the mind.

Eating something toxic can also disturb the body. The poor actions of people may get them into bad situations but, their overall outlook, vibe or aura makes you feel good when you're around them.

Artificial or Natural (continued)

We should never doubt ourselves to the point where we believe we cannot improve. If a mistake happens, one can just try to get back up, attempt to be better and not fall back into the same trap.

To look at life as a never-ending learning process and experience, may help us move ahead. If emotions are flat lined and hope is lost then everything begins to feel dull.

If the world were replaced with fake flowers, robots or people who never expressed and shared, the significance the world would be lost.

The bees would not be able to work miracles if only fake flowers existed. There would be no medicinal honey to make the world a sweeter place.

If the world was full of machines, nature would be destroyed. Too much technology is not in harmony with nature and causes the destruction of nature.

If people were never sincere, only insignificance would exist.

There would be no words filled with meaning, feeling, wisdom, sensitivity or spirituality.

Artificial or Natural (continued)

Fake is only a mirage of an external copy of the true and pure real meaning. If something is fake, there is no real rhythmic life in it.

Nature is real and a fake world can never hold the same significance as a natural raw, real world.

I don't want an artificial watermelon flavor. I need the watermelon that soaked up the sun, drunk the rain and lived in the soil.

What *Illusions* in life have damaged you?
Which ones do you struggle to let go off?

Flower Blues

By: Latifa Abdul-Haqq

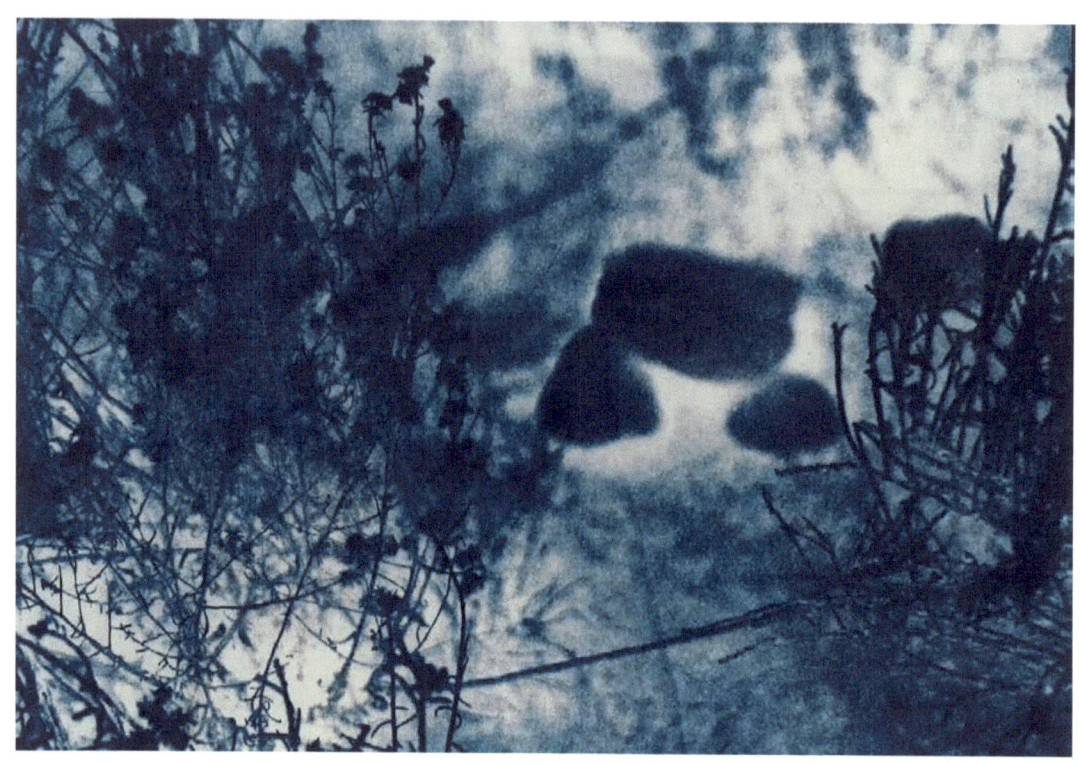

Marigolds

We leave severed pieces of our kindness as we find ourselves intermingling throughout the years.

We find ourselves miles apart or even in different time zones.

As the sun rises in my area, the sun sets into a gentle evening somber where you are.

As life unfolds untold, we find comfort in each other's warmest thoughts.

We laid out stepping stones for each other and that continues to build our friendship.

You cry and I collect your tears to water your garden.

When gray clouds of smoke fog my logic, you blow them away.

You say, "breathe" and then I am able to clear my head.

Hey, those bitter seeds we cared for, grew into bright Marigolds.

Love Bee
By: Jamilah Abdullah

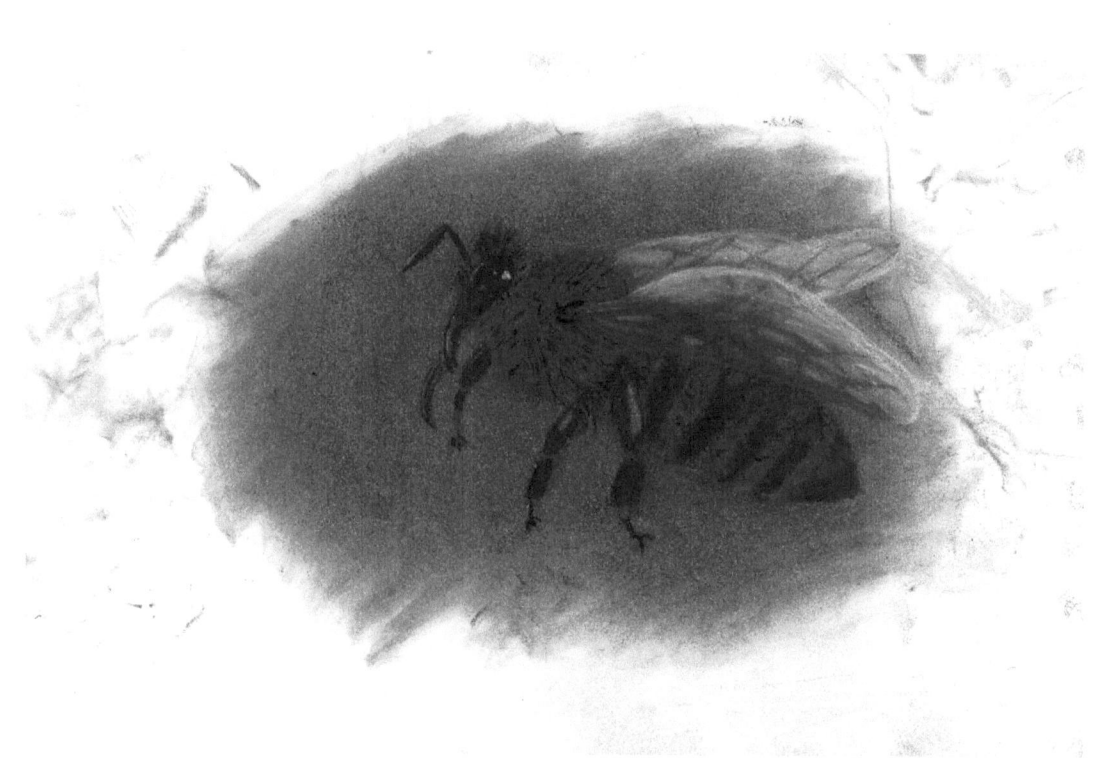

A Love Lost

Should you put her first
When the world
Around both of you
Gets like a whirlwind?

Will you love and cherish
The gifts now or will
You let them slip away
Like grains of sand?

Pouring out from
Between the
Fingers joined
To hand?

Will you take her hand
In yours and tell her
What you know in your
Heart to be true?

Will a love be lost or
Will it only grow?

A Love Lost (continued)

Shall we make our own sugar?
Should we know unconditional
Love, and find our riches
Without a dollar bill?

Even if there are no answers
Now, then look to life as
A mysterious journey only filled
With good.

While on the road to love, you can still find Yùgen by preparing yourself to be loved. That way, when you meet your significant other, you are ready to open up and give them your all.

That preparation depends on what each individual needs, but for many, it may mean really knowing yourself and what you want out of a relationship. If someone walks away from the love you have to give, then you have to let go. As broken hearted as you may feel, that person only saw you as a caterpillar and there is someone who will see you as the butterfly you are.

There is no need to stay in disappointment, because it is best to seek a healthy relationship than stay in a dysfunctional one just because you are afraid to fly.

What's your opinion regarding Love & *Yùgen?*

_____

_____

_____

_____

_____

_____

_____

_____

Bullhead & Pot
By: Jamilah Abdullah

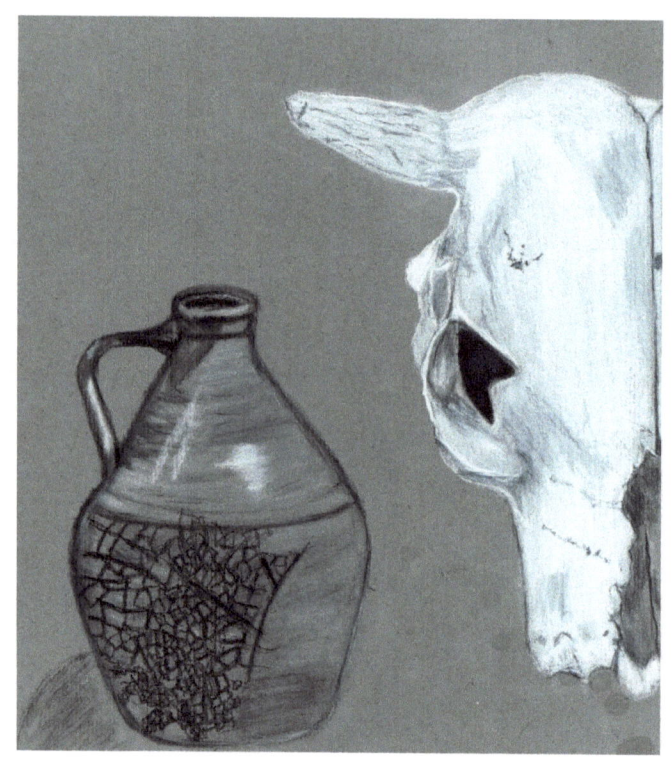

Blood Transaction

Sacrifice has been around
For as long as the word religion
Rang from mountaintops.

The bloodshed of a young lamb
Covers new ground
And cleanse the land of the dilapidated.

To Renew, one must let go,
And in doing so
Make way for the better that is about to
Spread through the person's life.

As the pulsing blood in the veins
Beat out the sound l-i-f-e
The only thing coursing through the mind is:
Trust!

Trust that as you cry out for help in the mountains…
The echoes that come back
Will reveal what his or her heart always
Remembered.

Southwest Sunset
By: Latifa Abdul-Haqq

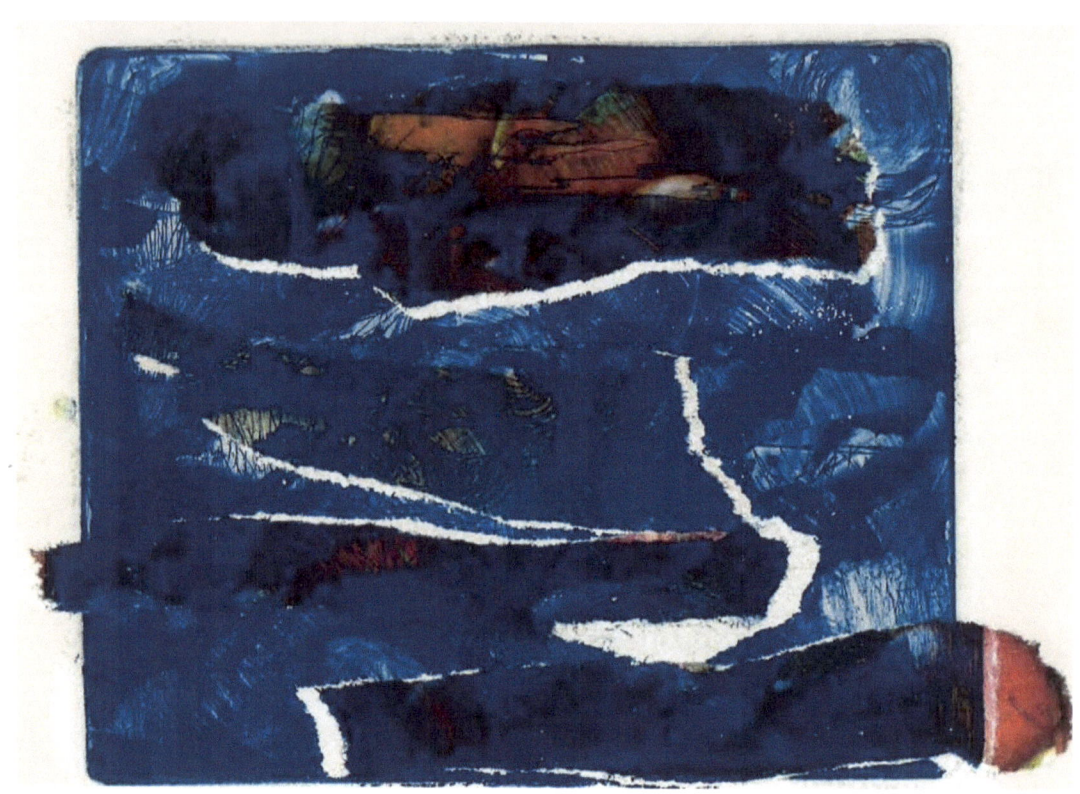

Pretty Things:

A pretty image is when light comes in rays through a window and cast itself upon the hands

      Or feet.

The sky that possesses the sun, stars, cloud, and planets

Fresh and reborn

Older women making bread from a grandmother's recipe

The moment a bird opens her wings to set flight

The landing of a leaf upon water.

Embarrassing Things:

Taking too long to notice the smell of a perfume on your own sleeve

Waving to someone you supposed was waving to you, when that person was

      Actually

      Waving to the passerby behind you.

Talking too much when everything has silenced for a good reason.

Earthy Things:

Roots in a glass of water

A pot of worms

Autumn grass

Pretty Things (continued):

Alone Things:

An epiphany

Meditation

A cave

A swim

A prayer

A breath.

What are the *pretty things* in your life?
What sacrifices have been made for them?

_____

_____

_____

_____

_____

_____

_____

_____

Sr. Owl
By: Jamilah Abdullah

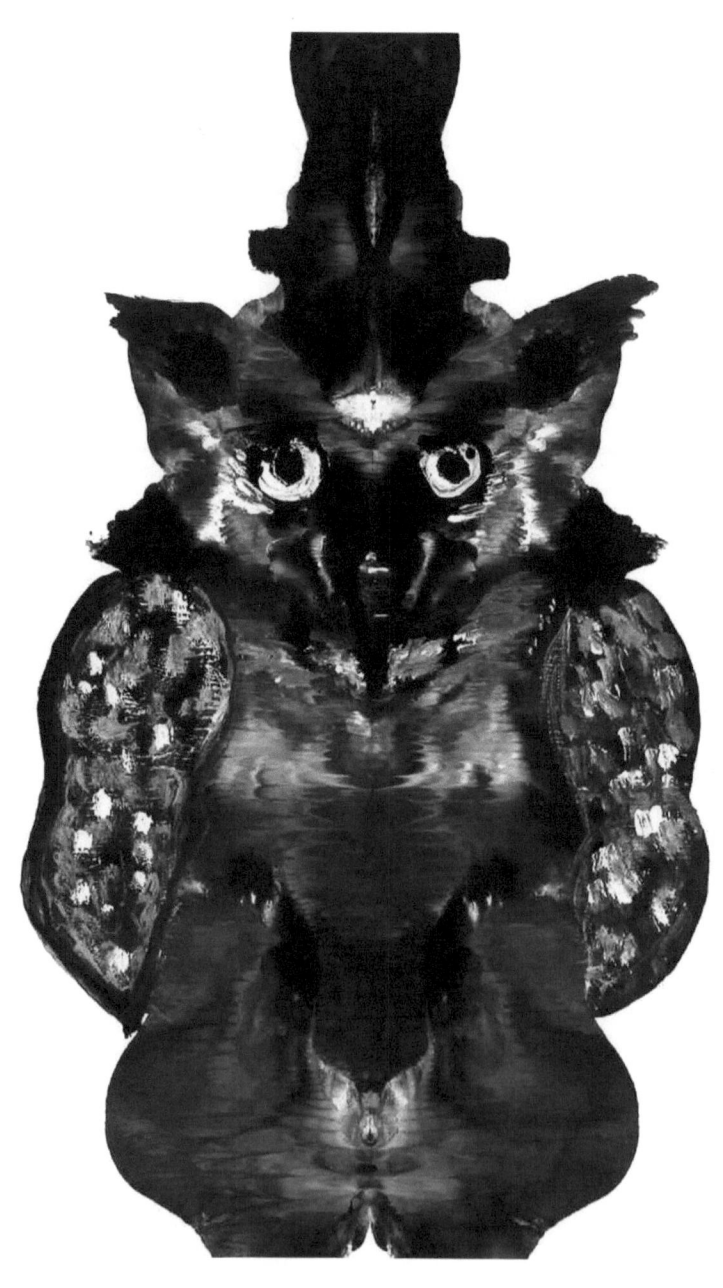

Tree Poem

Vines cling to a tree.

The tree exhales leaves all around.

The leaves whirl in the wind.

Rain finds a way through mingled branches.

The ground opens,   and spring rises.

Northern Lights
By: Jamilah Abdullah

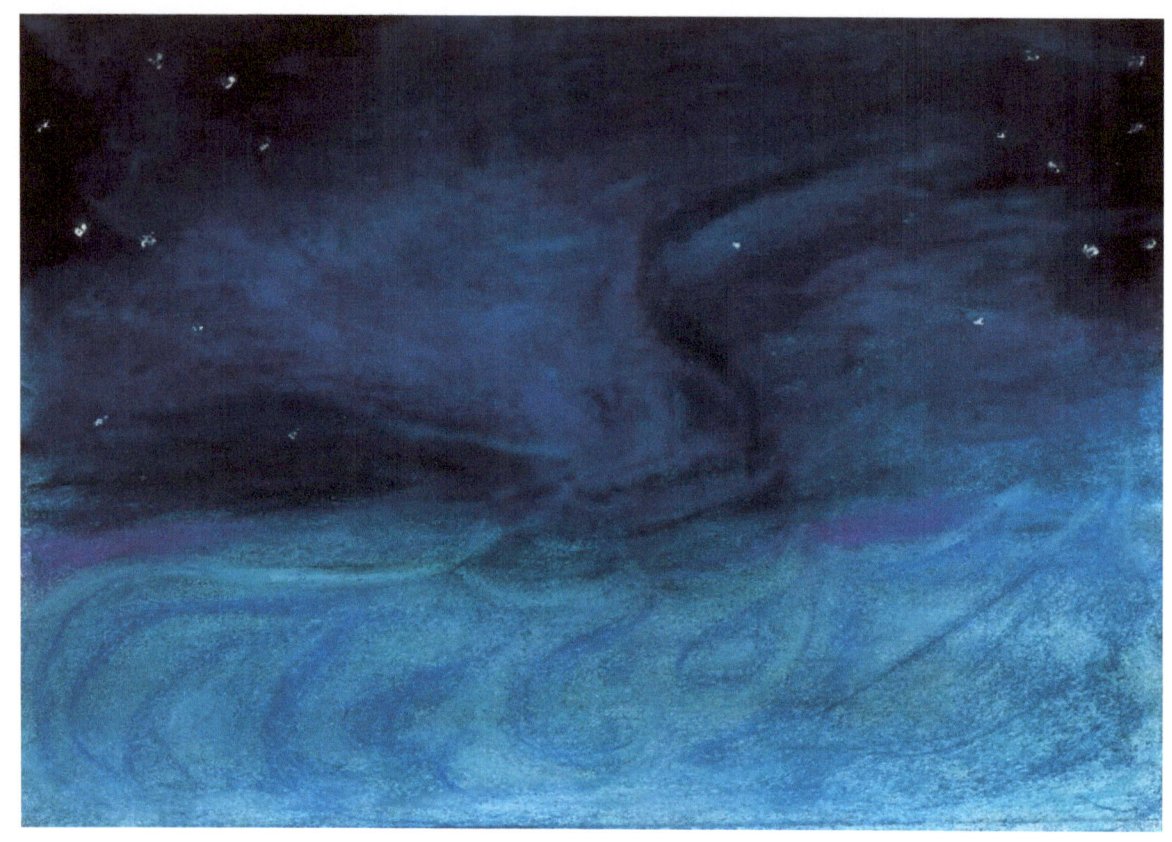

Link Verse

Swaying Spanish moss
A grayish purple night sky
Pine tree tops above.

Birthing Flower
By: Latifa Abdul-Haqq

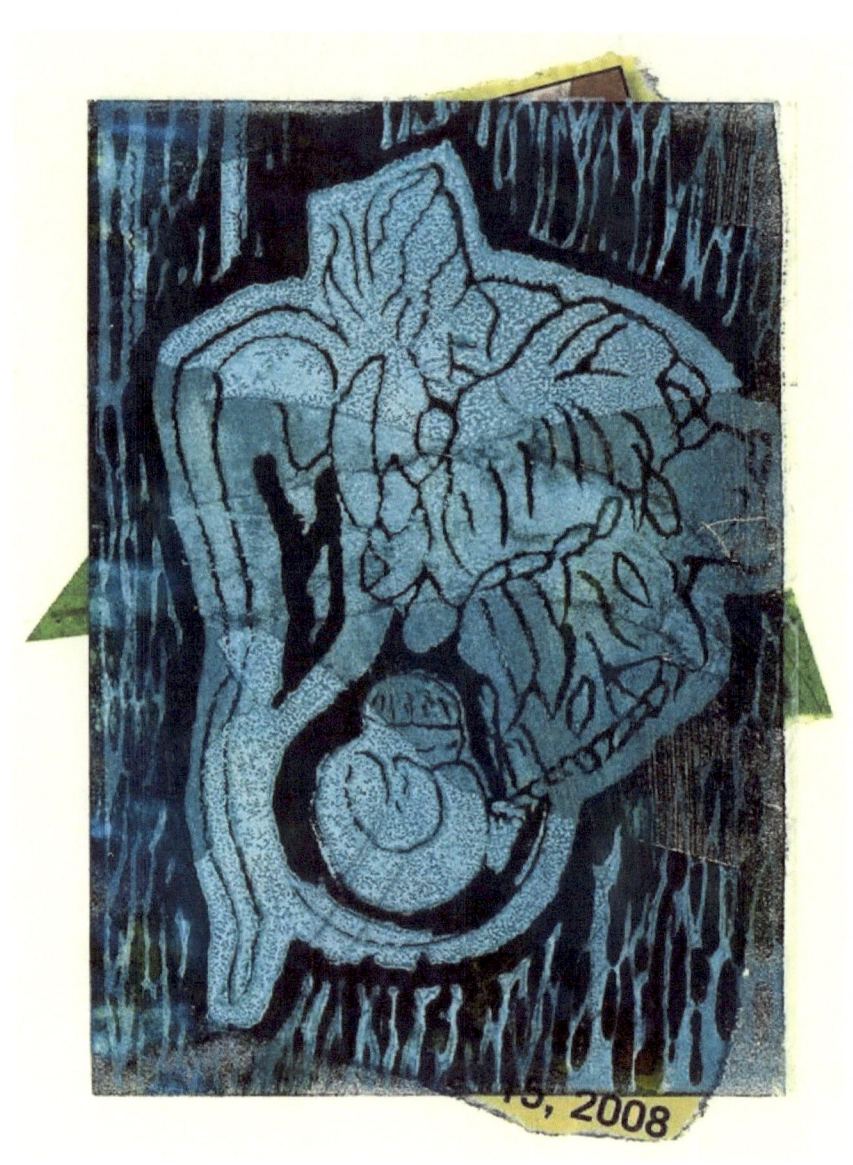

Jasmine Poem

Jasmine monsoon rain

Blossoms with hearted leaves

Luminous tree.

Bird Pie

By: *Jamilah Abdullah*

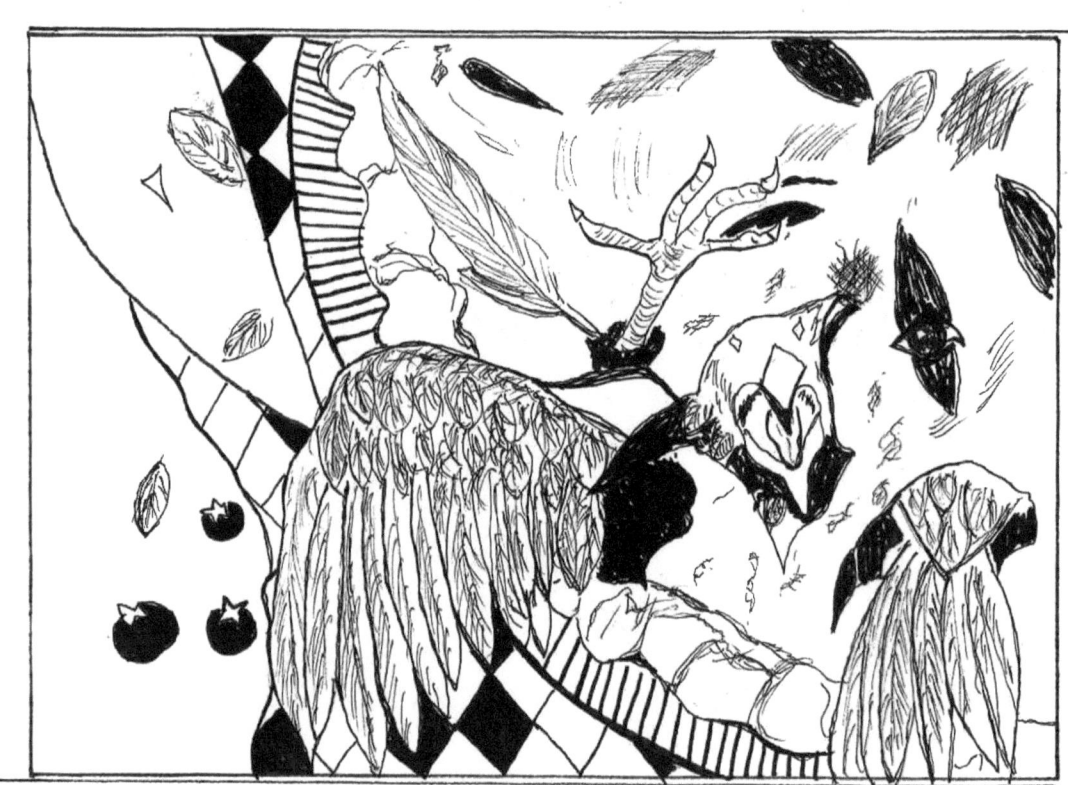

Wait For The Beat

I'm waiting to drink a new intake.
I'm waiting for a smack in the face.

I'm waiting for new people and forgotten ones to enter my life.

I'm waiting to take a cruise in a glass boat while watching fish full of omega 3's.

I'm waiting for red, yellow, and green balloons to be on my doorstep.

I'm waiting to really know the meaning of freestyle.

I'm waiting to hear a distant voice.
I'm waiting to float.

I'm waiting for you to tell me something.

— Now wait a minute —

The past is pushing me forward
And the future is pulling my hand,
And as the two merge within me
I feel what is now.

I wrote this poem my senior year of high school. I wrote this poem, at the time, to express the excitement and anticipation for the next step in my life.

This poem was on the back of my graduating class commencement brochure.

Apple Pin Cushion
By: Jamilah Abdullah

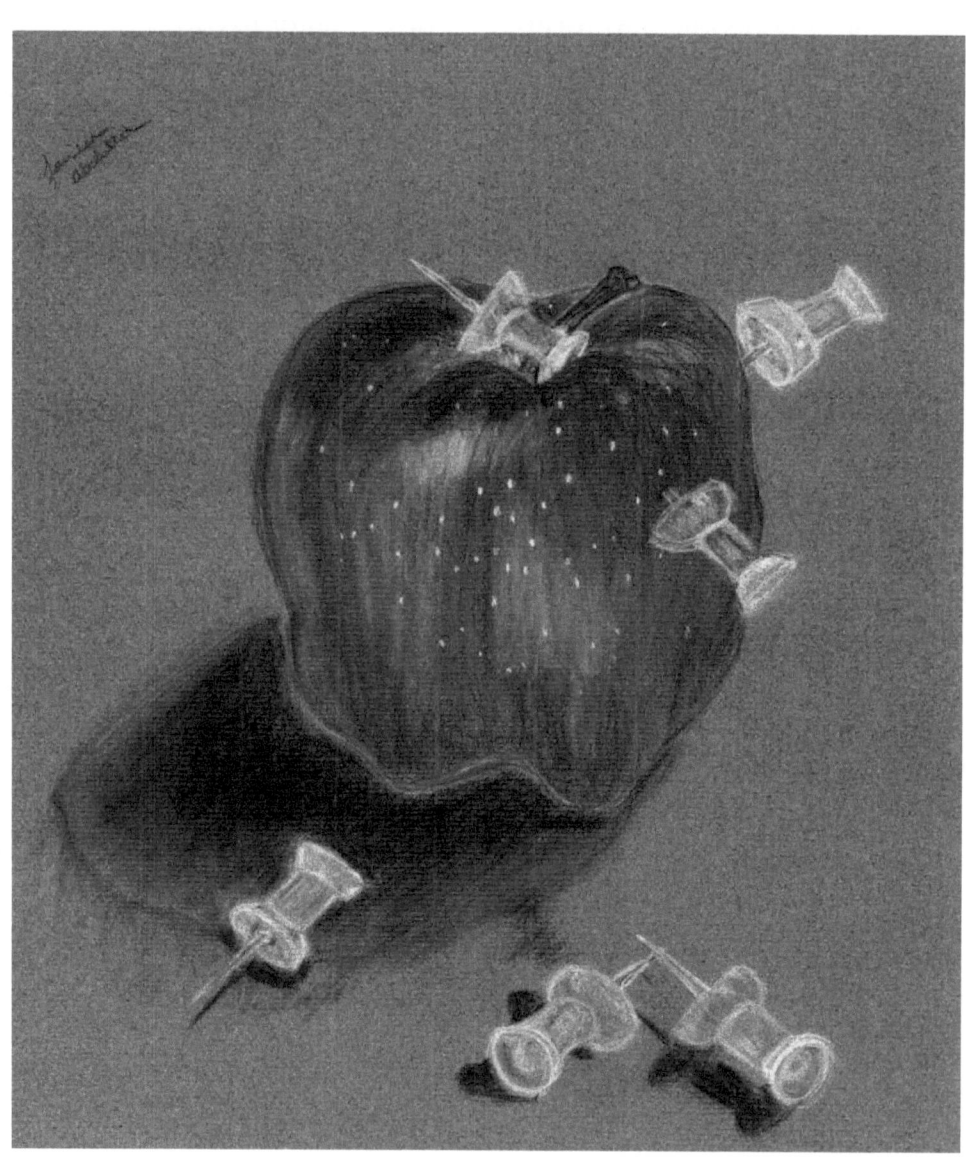

A Funny **Pun on the Mundane**

Disowning

Should I keep people around solely based on how useful they are to me? This is purely objectifying people. I am a type of person that does not like to own things that are not useful, so I find myself often giving things away. This notion does not simply apply to people.

What if people purely do just bless me with their presence? People interact with each other through conversation, stories, laughter, games, sports, cooking and, yes, eating – that good stuff we call *food*.

I can throw or give away things, but friendships and relationships are much harder to just toss out or pass along. They leave imprints on my heart and they change my outlook on aspects in life. The people I choose to keep in my life should help me to grow, even if I don't recognize the progress right away.

Men

Coffee is the best way I have found to describe men. All men are bitter, but they can give us women a pick-me-up like coffee. Some men have a little more sugar and cream in their cup, if you know what I mean. Men know that they're like tall cups of dark coffee and that women will come flocking once they are hooked. I do not feel guilty about referring to men as coffee because men use terms such as bag'em up, as if women are were some type of tea.

A Funny **Pun on the Mundane (Continued)**

Bosses off Duty

Why do some people feel the need to boss other people around after work hours? Bossiness is a characteristic most people do not like. People often do not mind advice or suggestions, but being told what to do cramps one's style.

There are different strokes for different folks. Look, if someone is not causing harm…that's their thing; let them do whatever floats their boat.

Let's not confuse bossiness with leadership. A leader can find a gift or skill in everyone and help them utilize it to the max to help the whole. Bossiness is believing one has some special ordained authority to order everyone else around to fulfill a vision they see.

Spirituality

To be a spiritual person can happen in many forms, but spirituality is formless. It does not just live in a mosque or temple or even holy water.

It can come along the vibration of the notes as a person dances alone in their bedroom. Spirituality can come as you hike to the top of a mountain and behold the night sky. Spirituality can come as you become one with the ocean. Spirituality is feeling lively and yet being at peace with the consciousness of the universe. We are all made from star dust and have our own energy we release to humanity.

A Funny **Pun on the Mundane (Continued)**

Bullying

A person who picks on another is often projecting their insecurity on another. They are trying to make the other person feel small, so that they can feel like a bigger person. Being a bigger person actually involves being able to compliment others and encourage them to succeed.

When a person boast, they are trying to look important. Mean jokes are a form of bullying, even if the person says, "just joking".

Bullying is also when girls outcast a specific girl, because that girl will not conform to the group. They may leave her out by not inviting her to certain events.

There is also the dress code. Girls use this dress code as a means to look down upon and outcast a particular girl. Girls in pairs can be best friends; girls in groups are like female lions on the prowl.

School

Learning is one of the most important and valuable aspects of human life. Education can go beyond the scope of a lecture followed by a writing assignment. A teacher can assign a project, use real life examples, show modern videos or students could interact with each other in small groups and play educational games like jeopardy.

Classes that I am most engaged in involve different activities. I end up retaining and actually learning instead of just memorizing and regurgitating.

A Funny **Pun on the Mundane (Continued)**

School (Continued)

The whole idea of college needs some reshaping. College has been built on the philosophy of survival of the fittest. The College system is known to weed people out. To survive, the number one rule is to be determined and work hard. As any student knows, in order to stay afloat, one has to hustle by finding the most efficient way to complete work.

What are some of your *Puns* on the Mundane?

_____

_____

_____

_____

_____

_____

_____

_____

Henna Fish

By: Jamilah Abdullah

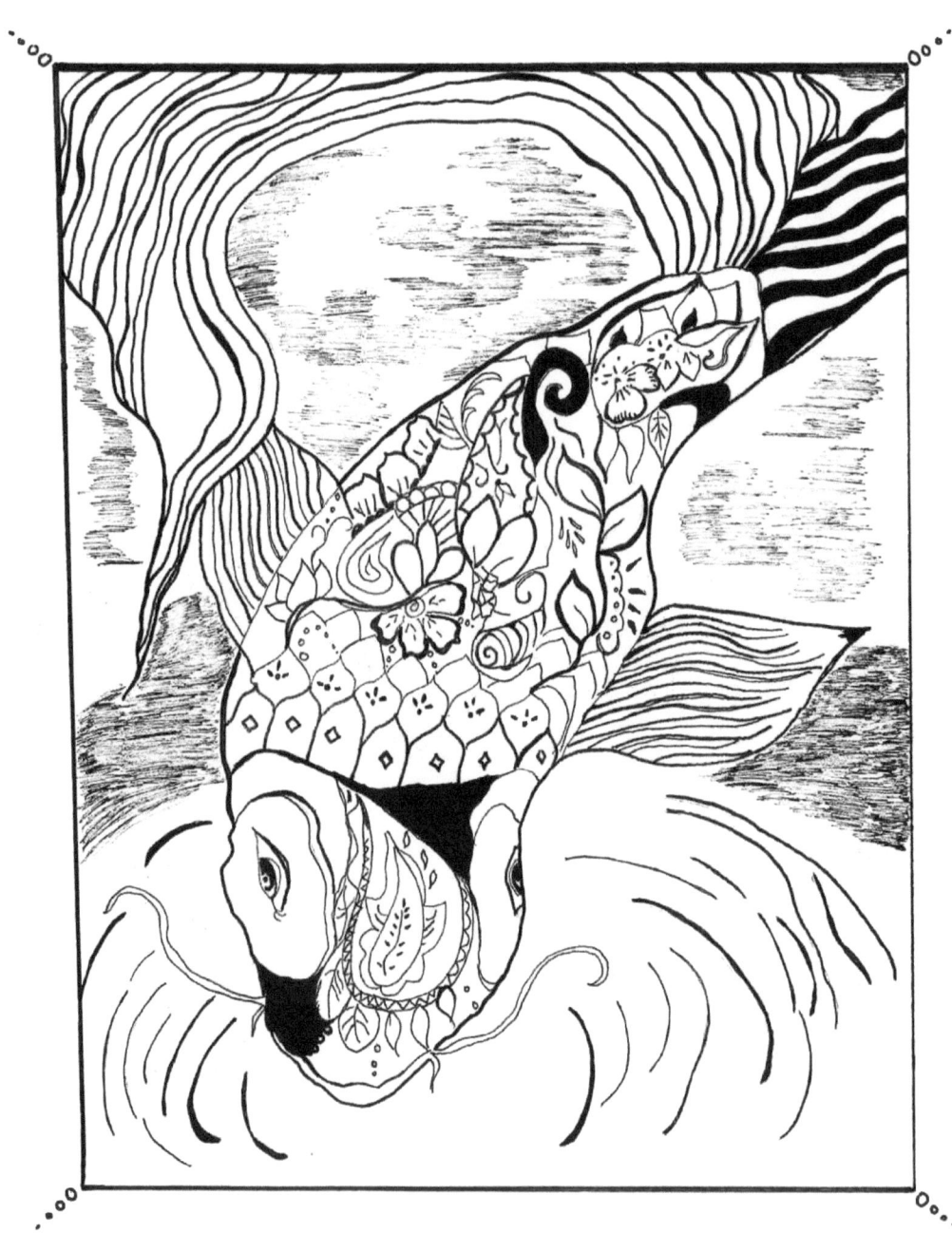

2:00 am

Pink lace like purple haze

Is something I like to call a mind boggler.

In the depth of the ocean, brain chemicals stir.

In the depth of the ocean, blue diamonds wait to be found.

As the sun sets upon every nation,

Every new generation

Blooms with inspiration.

Skull Mist

By: Jamilah Abdullah

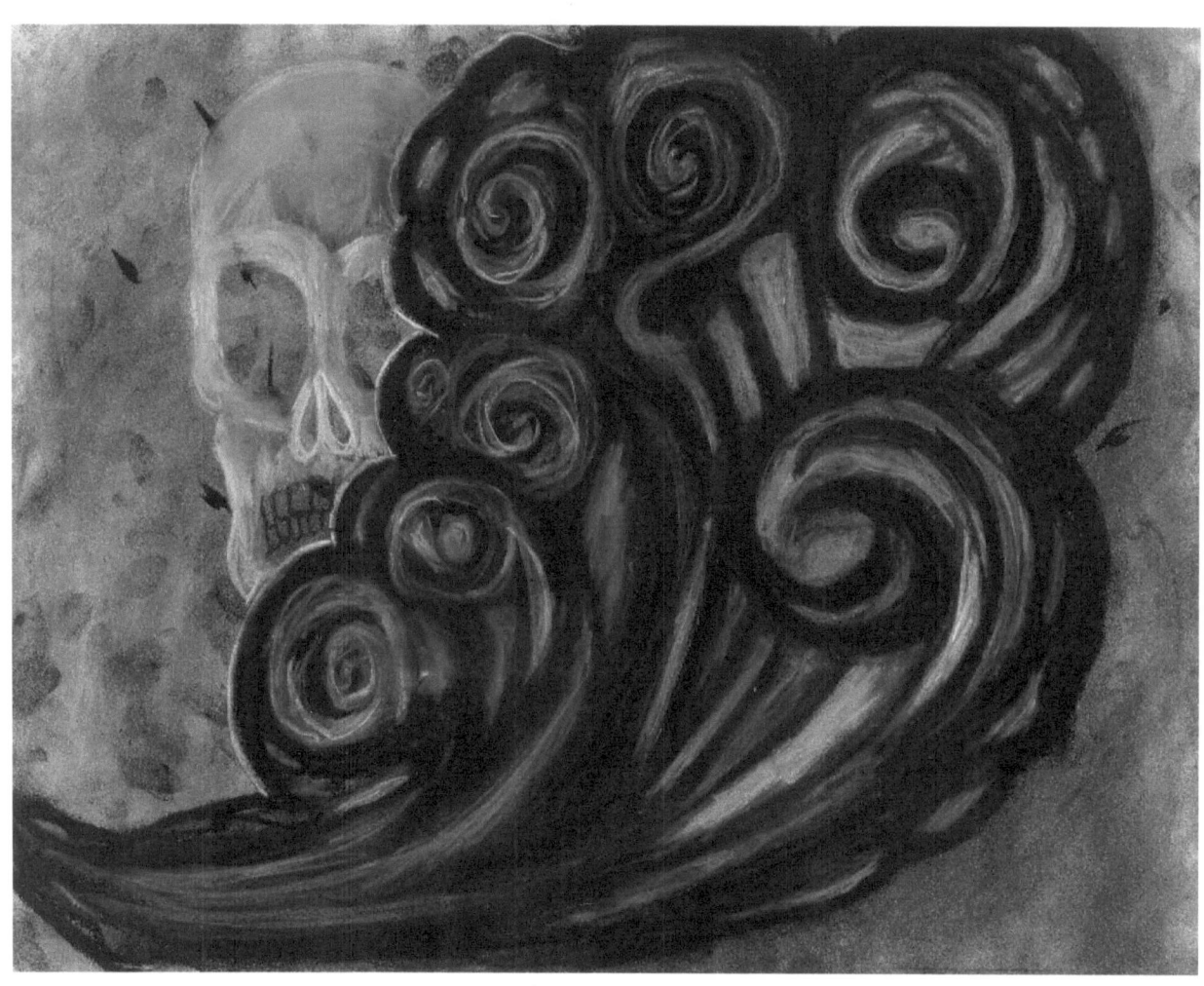

Dawn's

Dawn's solemn mist

Spreads over the ocean tides

The darkness vanished.

There are times when we feel somber but, just like the tide, things will change and get better. With an ounce of light in our hearts, the dark times will vanish.

This piece also represents having peace down to the core of our being by not harboring negative energy and channeling it into positive energy.

Rising Bird
By: Jamilah Abdullah

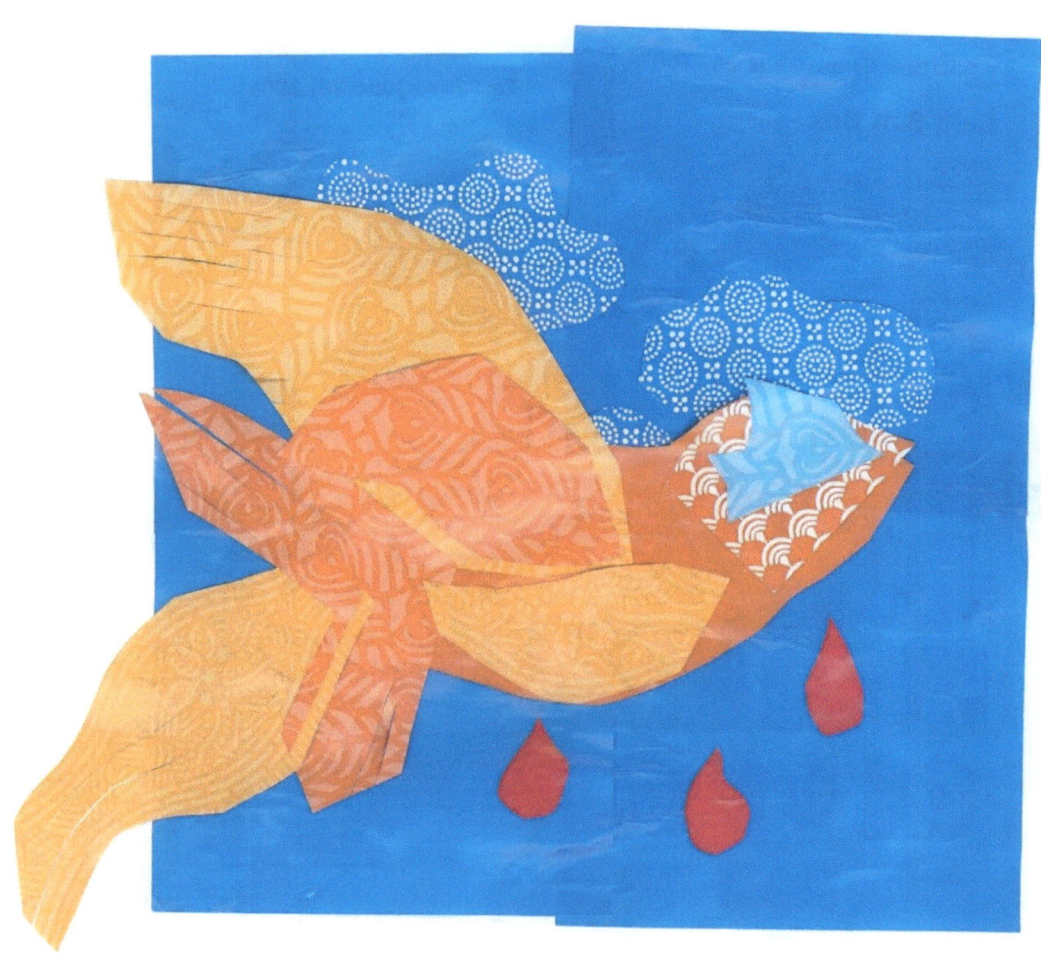

A Daydream

How many things are blank?

A blank paper, a blank wall, a blank stare

Or are we failing to see

All that is there.

The lines that are

Waiting for endless unspoken

Words of a civilization.

A wall bearing every family's

Secrets, traditions and testimonies of faith

Forms the structure of a home.

The blank stare often represents

A million things going on in the mind

Of a person lost in a daydream...

Explanation:

While daydreaming, a person might appear to be lost in space but are actually giving into their imagination.

Blankness is potential to create. Blank is part of the creative process; an artist starts with a blank canvas and writers start with a blank page. A house starts out empty until we fill it with laughter, love, and union, making it a home.

Blankness can stand for a fresh start. That means, even if you have hit rock bottom, it is your time to rise again. When you have a blank slate, you can come up with new ideas, goals and plans. Life is not over, just your old way of living and perception of life is.

What are your dreams and what are they trying to tell you?

_____

_____

_____

_____

_____

_____

_____

_____

Doorway
By: Latifa Abdul-Haqq

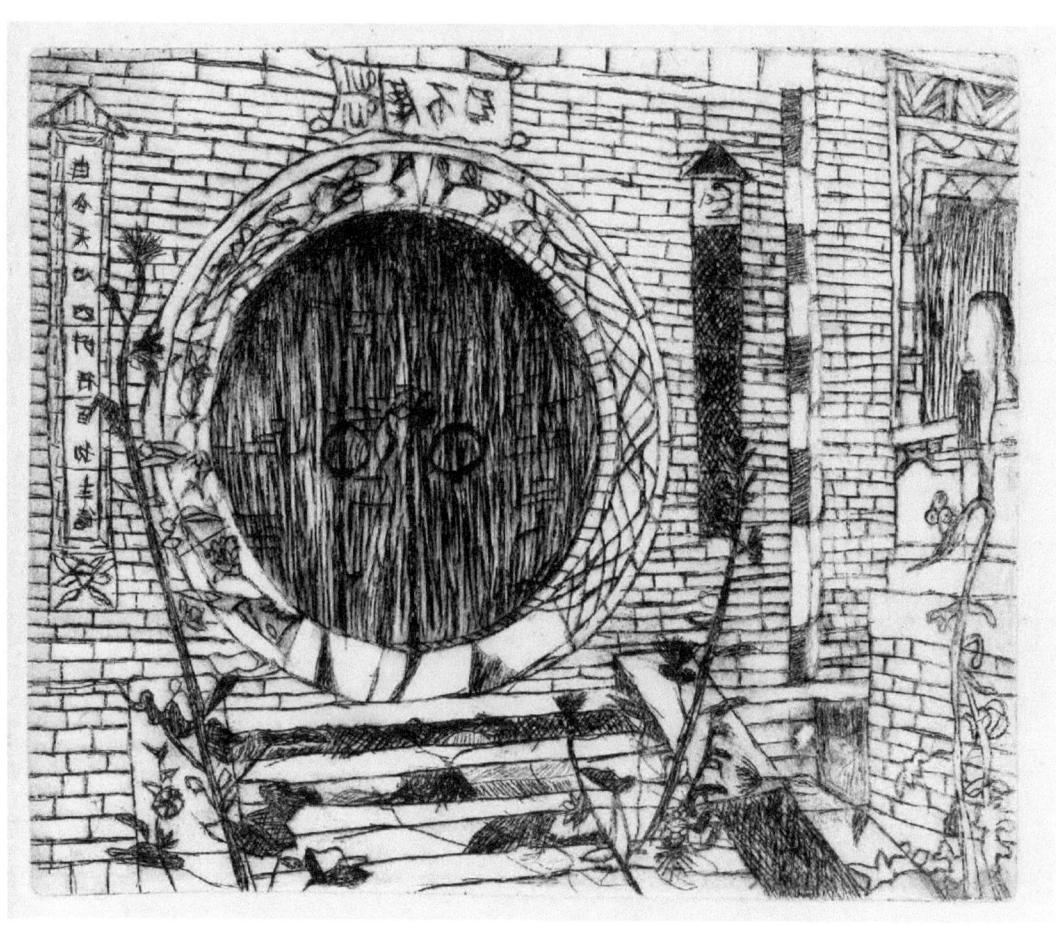

Open the Seal and Let the Light Wander Out

There is a fighting feeling
That wants to be
Free flowing on
The boat of joy.

It wants to be deepened
In passion.
It swirls around as
A new exciting light.

It calls to all the hearts
Who try to hide their
Feelings in a
Tightly sealed box.

Its enemies are those who
Do not believe.
It fights on with no will
To give up.

It wants to be heard,
It wants to be seen,
And, most of all,
It wants to be set free.

Explanation:

Think about the ways you have felt bound and wanted to break free but couldn't. What lessons did you learn in the process?

There are times when I feel trapped or stuck in a situation. And in these times, I have found that the most courageous thing to do is problem solve and work things out, instead of running for the nearest escape route.

What I have found is my shadow will follow me. I will always hear my thoughts and my feelings; they will manifest themselves no matter where I go on this earth.

As long as I live, I am a work in progress. Any time I feel dragged down by any type of bounds, belief is what gets me through. Belief that I am a valuable part of an intricate universe, and the belief that there is a higher power.

Contact/Follow Me

Through communication we form better relationships, share creative ideas and build culture.

The better we communicate, the better we function as a civilization. Working on expressing our inner voice through speech and writing, gives us the strength to live out loud.

Thank you for taking this journey with me. I hope that, through my selections of artwork and poetry, you have discovered the essence of beauty that can only be described as Yùgen.

If you would like to inquire about my artwork, poetry or to book me for a speaking engagement, please email: lujuabdull@gmail.com.

www.ingramcontent.com/pod-product-compliance
Lightning Source LLC
Chambersburg PA
CBHW050854180526
45159CB00007B/2669